rice &
risotto
perfection

HINKLER
BOOKS

rice &
risotto
perfection

Food Editor
Ellen Argyriou

Creative Director
Sam Grimmer

Project Editor
Lara Morcombe

First published in 2004 by Hinkler Books Pty Ltd
45–55 Fairchild Street
Heatherton Victoria Australia 3202
www.hinklerbooks.com
10 9 8 7 6

10 09 08

Disclaimer: The nutritional information listed under each recipe does not include the nutrient content of garnishes or
any accompaniments not listed in specific quantitites in the ingredient list. The nutritional information for each recipe
is an estimate only, and may vary depending on the brand of ingredients used, and due to natural biological variations
in the composition of natural foods such as meat, fish, fruit and vegetables. The nutritional information was calculated
by using Foodworks dietary analysis software (Version 3, Xyris Software Pty Ltd, Highgate Hill, Queensland, Australia)
based on the Australian food composition tables and food manufacturers' data. Where not specified, ingredients are
always analysed as average or medium, not small or large.

ISBN: 978-1-8651-5766-5

Printed and bound in China

contents

an introduction to rice

Labelled as 'one of the world's two most important food crops' rice is the staple food for a greater number of people than any other known plant. From its place of origin, it travelled to many lands and became embedded in the cuisines of many nations, creating the national dishes identified with them: the risottos of Italy, the paellas of Spain, the pilafs of the Middle East and the fried rice of many Asian and Southeast Asian countries. It is used in soups, salads, sweets, casseroles and curries. Rice has the ability to absorb other flavours, becoming what we want it to be. It is the most versatile of all grains and has been given the title of King of Kernels.

varieties of rice

There are about 60,000 varieties of rice cultivated around the world, but the most significant factor from the cook's standpoint is the shape and length of the grain and its starch content.

arborio rice: Has a large, plump, rounded kernel. It is grown in the Po Valley in Northern Italy. It has a high starch content, which gives the distinctive creamy texture to Italian risottos. It is also good for inclusion in soups and makes a creamy rice pudding.

basmati rice: Has a long, narrow kernel and is prized for its fragrance and nutty flavour. Originating in the foothills of the Himalayas, it is the preferred rice for Indian cooking. Its flavour and firm yet tender texture when cooked, has made it popular with all cuisines.

long-grain rice: Many varieties are produced under this title. They all have a long, thin kernel and remain well separated, dry and fluffy when cooked. The flavour is somewhat bland but its features make it the best choice for rice salads and for pilafs as it absorbs other flavours well.

short and medium grained rice: These varieties have a short, round kernel, some shorter than others. When cooked they are moist, slightly sticky and tend to cling. It is the rice to eat with chopsticks. They have a higher starch content than long-grained rice varieties, which makes them suitable as a thickener in soups; to use in stuffings for chicken, stuffed tomatoes and capsicums and vine leaf rolls; for moulded rice and sushi, rice cakes and patties; and, of course, a good rice custard or creamed rice.

brown rice: Most of the above varieties may be purchased in the brown form. Brown rice has the tough outer hull removed only, leaving the bran layer which covers the grain in tact. Because of the presence of this bran, brown rice is more nutritious than white and it takes longer to cook.

glutinous rice: Is a short-grained rice which when boiled becomes sweet and sticky with an appealing flavour. It is used as an ingredient in Asian sweets and snacks but not used for savoury dishes or as an accompanying table rice. Polished and unpolished black rice varieties are available.

cooking rice

how much?
1 cup of raw rice gives 3 cups of cooked rice. This quantity will serve 3–4 people.

Some cook rice by guess work, which can make it difficult to gain a good result. Based on how many serves you need to produce, calculate the amount of raw rice needed to be cooked and use one of the following methods, eg, for 6 serves of cooked rice 1$^1/_2$ cups of raw rice will need to be cooked.

boiling methods

rapid boil method: Rice is cooked in a large quantity of boiling, salted water for 12–15 minutes (30–35 minutes for brown rice) until soft but still firm at the core. It is then drained through a strainer. Use about 2 litres (3 pints) of water to 1 cup raw rice. This method ensures a separated, fluffy, dry grain; however, the liquid discarded takes some nutrients with it.

absorption method: Rice is cooked in a measured quantity of water, which will be absorbed by the rice. There is no loose water left to drain out so no nutrients are lost. Bring 2 cups (250 ml, 8 fl oz) water and a little salt to the boil and slowly stir in 1 cup rice. Cover tightly with a lid and turn down the heat to as low as possible. Simmer for 20 minutes without disturbing. Turn off heat or remove from hot plate and stand, without removing the lid for 5–8 minutes; the rice will plump up in the stored heat. Fluff up with a fork and serve immediately. Brown rice will need 45 minutes cooking and 10 minutes standing time.

pilaf method: Heat 2 tablespoons olive oil, ghee or butter in a heavy-based saucepan over moderate heat. Add 1 cup of rice and stir to coat all grains. Continue to stir over the heat about 2–3 minutes until the rice has a rosy tinge. Add 1½ cups (375 ml, 12 fl oz) boiling water and a little salt. Reduce heat to low and cover with a tight lid. Simmer 15 minutes for white rice and 40 minutes for brown. Turn off heat and stand covered for 5–8 minutes. Fluff up with a fork and serve.

microwave method: It will take the same amount of time to cook rice in the microwave as it will on the top of the stove. For small amounts it is convenient to use the microwave, for large amounts it is best to use a saucepan. Adding hot water to the rice will reduce time by about 5 minutes. Place 1 cup of rice and 2 cups (500 ml, 16 fl oz) hot water in a large microwave safe container. Cook on 100% power for 10–12 minutes. Stand covered for 5 minutes before removing cover.

reheating rice

1 Place the cooked rice in a colander over simmering water and heat through.

2 Place the cooked cold rice in a microwave safe dish, sprinkle with a little water and cover. Heat for 4–6 minutes on high power depending on the amount of rice and the wattage of the microwave oven.

preparing rice for fried rice

For a good result when making fried rice, the cooked rice must be free of moisture.

1 Cook the rice in advance, preferably the day before, for it takes time to remove the moisture.

2 Boil the rice by the rapid boil method, rinse well with cold water and leave to drain very well.

3 Spread the rice onto a shallow tray and place uncovered in the refrigerator for at least 2 hours; the cold air has a drying effect. Rake over the rice after 1 hour to bring the underside to the top.

4 For quick convenience keep prepared rice for frying in sealed bags in the freezer. It may be used in the frozen state.

flavouring rice

It is easy to flavour the rice while cooking it to make tasty accompaniments.

quantities:
1 cup (200 g, 7 oz) long or medium grained rice
1 cup (250 ml, 8 fl oz) liquid

method used:
absorption method: Place all ingredients in a saucepan, bring to the boil stirring occasionally. Turn down heat to a simmer, cover with a lid and simmer for 20 minutes. Stand covered for 5–8 minutes before removing lid to serve.

apple rice:
1 cup rice, 1 cup (250 ml, 8 fl oz) apple juice, 1 cup (250 ml, 8 fl oz) stock or water, 1 tart apple (finely diced), salt to taste. Serve with pork.

lemon rice:
1 cup rice, 1³/₄ cups (440 ml, 14 fl oz) water, 4 tablespoons lemon juice, 1 teaspoon grated lemon rind, 1 cup (250 ml, 8 fl oz) stock or water, 2 tablespoons sultanas, salt to taste. Serve with fish.

orange rice:
1 cup rice, 1 cup (250 ml, 8 fl oz) orange juice, 2 teaspoons grated orange rind, 1 cup (250 ml, 8 fl oz) stock or water, 2 tablespoons sultanas, salt to taste. Serve with chicken.

onion rice:
1 cup rice, ¹/₂ packet dried onion soup mix, 2 cups (500 ml, 16 fl oz) water. No salt needed. Serve with steaks.

starters, soups and salads

california rolls

ingredients

4 green prawns, peeled and deveined
2 sheets nori seaweed
1 1/2 cup (280 g, 9 oz) prepared sushi rice,
    see opposite
30 g (1 oz) shredded lettuce
1 small cucumber, cut into strips,
    lengthwise
1/2 avocado, sliced
1 tablespoon flying fish roe or red caviar
1 1/2 tablespoons mayonnaise
makes 16

> **i**
>
> **preparation time**
> 10 minutes
>
> **cooking time**
> 1 minute
>
> **nutritional value
> per serve**
> fat: 6 g
> carbohydrate: 13.6 g
> protein: 5.3 g

1 Cook prawns in boiling water for 1 minute, remove and place in iced water immediately. Slice in half lengthwise.

2 Place nori sheet, shiny side down, on a bamboo mat. Spread over 1/2 of the rice, leaving a 2 cm margin along top end of seaweed. Place half the prawns, lettuce, cucumber, avocado, flying fish roe or red caviar and mayonnaise across the rice 4 cm in from front edge.

3 Lifting the mat, place the front strip of rice over the filling. Press lightly along the seam then pull the mat towards the top end, rolling the sushi into a tight roll as you pull. Remove bamboo mat and make a second roll.

4 Using a wet, sharp knife, cut roll into 8 even-sized pieces.

sushi rice

ingredients

1/2 cup (110 g, 3 1/2 oz) short-grain rice
1 cup (250 ml, 8 fl oz) water
1 tablespoon rice vinegar or white-
    wine vinegar
1/2 teaspoon salt
1 teaspoon sugar
yields 1 1/2 cups (280 g, 9 oz)

1 Wash rice in 2 or 3 changes of water until water runs clear.

2 Place rice in a saucepan with the water. Bring to the boil, reduce heat and simmer covered for 12–15 minutes until water has absorbed. Remove from heat and stand covered for 10 minutes.

3 In a bowl, stir the vinegar, salt and sugar to dissolve the sugar. Place the rice in a flat-based dish. Run the side of a spatula criss-cross through the rice drizzling over the vinegar and continuing the slashing motion. Fan the top of the rice, then toss up from the base to release the heat. Cover with a damp cloth until ready to use.

> **i**
>
> **preparation time**
> 15 minutes
>
> **cooking time**
> 18 minutes
>
> **nutritional value
> per serve**
> fat: 1 g
> carbohydrate: 15 g
> protein: 6 g

salmon box sushi

ingredients

1 kelp sheet
$^1/_2$ cup (125 ml, 4 fl oz) rice vinegar
250 g (8 oz) fresh salmon, cut into 5 mm thick slices
5 shiso leaves, cut into 5 mm strips or use fresh basil leaves
3 cups (560 g, 18 oz) prepared sushi rice (see page 12)

makes 8

preparation time
5 minutes, plus
4 hours or
overnight
standing

cooking time
10 minutes

nutritional value per serve
fat: 2.3 g
carbohydrate: 19.1 g
protein: 7.4 g

1 Simmer kelp in rice vinegar for 5–10 minutes, until soft. Wet a wooden sushi mould or line a rectangular container measuring 25 x 7.5 x 6 cm high (bar tin) with clingwrap. Allow the clingwrap to overhang by at least 10 cm each side.

2 Arrange $^1/_3$ of the salmon over the base of the mould to cover. Sprinkle over $^1/_3$ of the shiso leaves. Spoon over 1$^1/_2$ cups (280 g, 9 oz) rice and gently press down. Repeat with $^1/_3$ salmon, $^1/_3$ shiso, remaining rice and remaining salmon and shiso. Top with strips of cooked kelp.

3 Place the wet wooden lid on the mould, or cover with overhanging clingwrap. Place a weight on top and leave for at least 4 hours, or overnight.

4 Carefully remove the compressed sushi from the mould and unwrap. Using a wet, sharp knife, cut into 8 equal portions and serve.

dolmades

ingredients

500 g (1 lb) packet preserved vine
   leaves, rinsed
3/4 cup (170 ml, 5 1/2 fl oz) olive oil
2 large onions, finely chopped
1 cup (220 g, 7 1/2 oz) short-grain rice
2 tablespoons pine nuts
2 tablespoons finely chopped parsley
2 tablespoons finely chopped mint
3 tablespoons currants
salt and pepper
2 cups (500 ml, 16 fl oz) water
juice of 1 lemon
makes 60–65

1 Into a saucepan of boiling
water, drop 1/3 of the vine
leaves for 2 minutes. Remove
to a bowl of cold water. Repeat
with remainder. Drain well and
separate out onto a large
kitchen cloth.

2 Heat 2 tablespoons of oil in
a large saucepan and gently
fry the onions until coloured.
Add the rice and pine nuts and
stir 2 minutes. Add the parsley,
mint, currants, salt, pepper and
1 cup (250 ml, 8 fl oz) water.
Cover and cook over medium
heat for 15 minutes or until all
water is absorbed.

i

preparation time
30 minutes

cooking time
1 hour 20 minutes

**nutritional value
per serve**
fat: 14.2 g
carbohydrate: 8.1 g
protein: 2.5 g

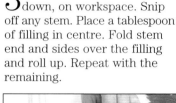

3 Place a leaf, smooth side
down, on workspace. Snip
off any stem. Place a tablespoon
of filling in centre. Fold stem
end and sides over the filling
and roll up. Repeat with the
remaining.

4 Line a large heavy-based
saucepan with left over vine
leaves. Pack a layer of rolls seam
side down and sprinkle with a
little of the remaining oil and
some of the lemon juice. Pack
a second and third (if needed)
layer on top, sprinkling each
with oil and lemon juice. Add
the remaining cup of water.
Invert a plate on top of the rolls
to prevent unravelling. Bring to
the boil, turn heat down, cover
and simmer for 1 hour. Remove
from heat, stand covered for 1
hour to absorb the liquid. Lift
rolls carefully onto a platter,
garnish with lemon. Serve
chilled or at room temperature.

curried rice with smoked haddock

ingredients

360 g (12 oz) smoked haddock,
  cut into 3 pieces
1 tablespoon olive oil
2 tablespoons butter
1 onion, chopped
2 sticks celery, sliced
1 green chilli, deseeded and
  finely chopped
$^1/_2$ teaspoon ground turmeric
1 tablespoon mild curry powder
280 g (9 oz) basmati rice
900 ml ($1^1/_2$ pints) fish stock
4 tomatoes, skinned, deseeded
  and diced
400 g (13 oz) can chickpeas, drained
75 g ($2^1/_2$ oz) frozen baby green peas
4 tablespoons chopped fresh parsley
black pepper
2 lemons, cut into wedges
serves 4

1 Soak the haddock in cold water for 10 minutes. Change water and soak again for 10 minutes, drain. Place the haddock in a saucepan of boiling water. Simmer, covered, for 3–4 minutes, until the flesh starts to flake away from the skin. Lift out haddock and set aside.

2 Heat the oil and butter in a large heavy-based frying pan. Fry the onion, celery and chilli for 5 minutes. Add the turmeric, curry powder, rice and stock. Simmer, covered, for 10 minutes or until almost all the stock is absorbed, stirring from time to time.

3 Flake the fish, discarding the skin and bones. Stir into the rice with the diced tomatoes, chickpeas, baby green peas, parsley and pepper. Cook, uncovered, for 5 minutes or until everything is heated through. Serve with lemon wedges.

i

preparation time
15 minutes, plus
20 minutes
soaking

cooking time
25 minutes

**nutritional value
per serve**
fat: 1.9 g
carbohydrate: 5.7 g
protein: 4.7 g

tomatoes yemistes

ingredients

12 medium-sized ripe tomatoes, washed
2 teaspoons sugar
salt and pepper
extra 1/2 teaspoon sugar
1/2 cup (125 ml, 4 fl oz) olive oil
1 large onion, finely chopped
45 g (1 1/2 oz) pine nuts
1 1/4 cups (280 g, 9 oz) short-grain rice
75 g (2 1/2 oz) currants
1 1/2 cups (375 ml, 12 fl oz) hot water
2 tablespoons chopped flat-leaf parsley
2 tablespoons chopped mint
makes 12

1 Slice the top of each tomato almost through. Flip back the lid and scoop out the pulp with a teaspoon. Sprinkle each cavity with a pinch of sugar, place in a baking dish and set aside. Into a saucepan, place tomato pulp with salt, pepper and 1/2 teaspoon sugar. Simmer until pulp is soft. Press through a sieve, discard seeds. Set purée aside.

2 In a saucepan, heat 4 tablespoons oil and fry the onion until soft. Add pine nuts

and stir 2 minutes. Add rice, stir a little to coat grains. Add currants, hot water, parsley, mint and 1/2 cup (125 ml, 4 fl oz) tomato purée. Bring to the boil, turn down heat, cover and simmer gently 10–12 minutes, until all liquid is absorbed.

3 Preheat oven to 180°C (350° F, gas mark 4). Spoon rice mixture into tomatoes, allowing a little room for rice to swell. Replace lid. Pour remaining tomato purée over the tomatoes and add about 1/2 cup (125 ml, 4 fl oz) water to the dish.

4 Spoon remaining oil over the tomatoes and place, uncovered, into oven for 40–60 minutes or until rice is tender. Check liquid, if drying out, add a little extra water. Serve tomatoes with their sauce.

i

preparation time
25 minutes
cooking time
1 hour
nutritional value per serve
fat: 7.1 g
carbohydrate: 5.5 g
protein: 1.4 g

rice cakes with lime crab

ingredients

2 cups (370 g, 12 oz) cooked jasmine rice
2 tablespoons chopped coriander
crushed black peppercorns
vegetable oil for deep-frying
lime crab topping
185 g (6 oz) canned crab meat,
  well-drained
2 fresh red chillies, deseeded and
  chopped
2 small fresh green chillies, finely sliced
4 tablespoons coconut cream
2 tablespoons natural yoghurt
3 teaspoons lime juice
3 teaspoons thai fish sauce
3 teaspoons finely grated lime rind (zest)
1 tablespoon crushed black peppercorns
makes 24

1 In a bowl, combine rice, coriander and black peppercorns to taste. Press into an oiled 18 x 28 cm shallow cake tin and refrigerate until set. Cut rice mixture into 3 x 4 cm rectangles.

2 Heat vegetable oil (about 2½ cm deep) in a large frying pan until a cube of bread dropped in browns in 50 seconds. Cook rice cakes, a few at a time, for 3 minutes or until golden, turning once. Drain on absorbent paper.

3 In a food processor, place crab meat, red and green chillies, coconut cream, yoghurt, lime juice and fish sauce and process until smooth. Stir in lime rind and black peppercorns. Serve with warm rice cakes.

i

preparation time
20 minutes

cooking time
10–12 minutes

**nutritional value
per serve**
fat: 24.9 g
carbohydrate: 11.9 g
protein: 3.9 g

crispy rolls

ingredients

1 cup (220 g, 7½ oz) short-grain brown
   rice, cooked
125 g (4 oz) cooked chicken,
   finely chopped
4 spring onions (green onions), chopped
1 carrot, grated
30 g (1 oz) bean sprouts
30 g (1 oz) button mushrooms, chopped
4 canned water chestnuts, drained
   and chopped
1 tablespoon oyster sauce
1 tablespoon soy sauce
2 teaspoons white wine
1 teaspoon sugar
¼ teaspoon sesame oil
24 spring roll or wonton wrappers,
   each 12.5 cm square
vegetable oil for deep-frying
makes about 24

i

preparation time
20 minutes

cooking time
20 minutes

nutritional value
per serve
fat: 28.1 g
carbohydrate: 11.2 g
protein: 5.3 g

1 In a bowl, place rice, chicken, spring onions, carrot, bean sprouts, mushrooms, chestnuts, oyster and soy sauce, wine, sugar and sesame oil and mix well to combine. Take a spring roll wrapper, place on work surface with a corner tip to the front. Place a tablespoon of filling in the centre of each wrapper, fold one corner over filling, then tuck in the sides and roll up, sealing with water.

2 Heat vegetable oil in a deep-frying pan to 180°C (350°F, gas mark 4) or until a cube of bread browns in 50 seconds. Cook a few rolls at a time for 3–4 minutes or until golden. Remove rolls with a slotted spoon, drain on absorbent paper and serve immediately.

thai rice soup with chicken

ingredients

¹/₂ cup (110 g, 3¹/₂ oz) short-grain rice
1.25 litres (2 pints) water
1 tablespoon vegetable oil
1 large clove garlic, finely chopped
1 tablespoon finely grated fresh ginger
250 g (8 oz) chicken thigh or breast
   fillets, sliced 1 cm thick
white pepper to taste
2 tablespoons fish sauce
1 small onion, finely sliced
2 tablespoons chopped fresh coriander
2 tablespoons chopped spring onions
   (green onions)
extra fresh coriander for garnish
red chillies, finely sliced for garnish
extra spring onions, sliced for garnish
serves 4

1 In a large saucepan, place rice with the water and bring slowly to the boil. Boil gently for 30 minutes. Turn off the heat and stand covered for 10 minutes or until the mixture has a thin porridge consistency.

2 In a wok or large frying pan, heat the oil and stir-fry the garlic and ginger. Add the chicken, pepper, fish sauce and onion and stir-fry about 5 minutes until chicken is cooked. Stir into the rice stock. Just before serving stir in the coriander and spring onions. Ladle into heated bowls and garnish each with a few coriander leaves, chillies and spring onions.

preparation time
10 minutes

cooking time
40 minutes

nutritional value per serve
fat: 7.8 g
carbohydrate: 18.4 g
protein: 15.5 g

gingered thai rice salad

ingredients

2 cups (400 g, 13 oz) long-grain rice
1.5 litres (2½ pints) water
5 spring onions (green onions), finely sliced on the diagonal
3 medium carrots, coarsely grated
4 baby bok choy (pak choi), chopped
2 kaffir lime leaves, finely sliced
2 handfuls coriander, coarsely chopped
250 g (8 oz) roasted peanuts, chopped
1 tablespoon black sesame seeds
2 tablespoons chopped thai basil

dressing

2 tablespoons vegetable or peanut oil
3 tablespoons lime juice
3 tablespoons thai fish sauce
2 tablespoons palm sugar
2 tablespoons sweet chilli sauce
1 tablespoon finely chopped ginger
1 pinch chilli powder or cayenne pepper
salt and pepper to taste

serves 12

i

preparation time
15 minutes

cooking time
15 minutes

nutritional value per serve
fat: 7.5 g
carbohydrate: 21 g
protein: 5.2 g

1 Cook rice in boiling salted water for 10–12 minutes or until tender. Drain and rinse thoroughly in cold water then drain again. In a bowl, whisk together dressing ingredients and set aside.

2 In a separate bowl, combine spring onions, carrots, bok choy, lime leaves, coriander, peanuts and sesame seeds.

3 Add the cooked rice and mix well. Toss thoroughly with the dressing, add thai basil and serve.

greek orzo salad with olives and capsicums

ingredients

350 g (11½ oz) orzo or rice-shaped
  pasta
180 g (6 oz) feta cheese, crumbled
1 red capsicum (pepper), finely chopped
1 yellow capsicum, finely chopped
1 green capsicum, finely chopped
190 g (6½ oz) pitted kalamata olives,
  chopped
4 spring onions, sliced
2 tablespoons capers

dressing
juice and rind (zest) of 2 lemons
1 tablespoon white-wine vinegar
1 tablespoon finely chopped garlic
1½ teaspoons dried oregano
1 teaspoon dijon mustard
1 teaspoon ground cumin
100 ml (3½ fl oz) olive oil
salt and pepper
3 tablespoons pine nuts, toasted
serves 4-6

preparation time
15 minutes

cooking time
15 minutes

**nutritional value
per serve**
fat: 13 g
carbohydrate: 22 g
protein: 6.3 g

1 Cook the orzo in a large pot of boiling salted water until tender but still firm to bite. Drain and rinse with cold water. In a large bowl, place orzo with a little olive oil from the dressing ingredients.

2 Add the feta cheese, capsicums, olives, spring onions and capers.

3 In a small bowl, whisk together the lemon juice and rind, vinegar, garlic, oregano, mustard and cumin. Gradually add the remaining olive oil then season to taste with salt and pepper.

4 Drizzle the dressing over the salad and toss thoroughly. Garnish with the toasted pine nuts.

seafood

seafood and broccoli risotto

ingredients

1 tablespoon sunflower oil
6 spring onions (green onions), chopped
1 clove garlic, finely chopped
1 red or yellow capsicum (pepper), diced
225 g (7½ oz) long-grain brown rice
2 cups (500 ml, 16 fl oz) vegetable stock
225 g (7½ oz) chestnut mushrooms, sliced
1 cup (250 ml, 8 fl oz) dry white wine
400 g (13 oz) marinara mix or frozen seafood mix, defrosted
225 g (7½ oz) broccoli, cut into small florets and boiled for 3 minutes
2 tablespoons chopped flat-leaf parsley
salt and black pepper

serves 4

i

preparation time
15 minutes

cooking time
40 minutes

nutritional value per serve
fat: 1.7 g
carbohydrate: 10 g
protein: 5.9 g

1 Heat the oil in a large saucepan. Add the spring onions, garlic and capsicum and cook for 5 minutes or until softened, stirring occasionally. Add the rice and cook for 1 minute, stirring, until well

coated in the oil. In a separate saucepan, bring the stock to the boil.

2 Add the mushrooms, wine and ½ cup (125 ml, 4 fl oz) boiling stock to the rice mixture. Bring to the boil, stirring, then simmer, uncovered, for 15 minutes or until most of the liquid is absorbed, stirring often. Add another ¾ cup (185 ml, 6 fl oz) stock and cook for 15 minutes or until it is absorbed, stirring frequently.

3 Add the seafood and most of the remaining stock. Stir frequently for 5 minutes or until the rice is cooked but firm to the bite. Add the rest of the stock, if necessary, and make sure the seafood is cooked through. Stir in the remaining broccoli, parsley, salt and pepper. Serve immediately.

thai chilli tuna risotto

ingredients

2 tablespoons peanut oil
½ bunch spring onions (green onions), chopped
250 g (8 oz) button mushrooms, sliced
2 handfuls fresh coriander, chopped
2 tablespoons fish sauce
2 tablespoons lime juice
400 g (13 oz) arborio rice
150 ml (5 fl oz) white wine
1 litre (1 ⅔ pints) vegetable or fish stock
200 g (7 oz) oyster mushrooms
400 g (13 oz) can tuna with chilli
1 handful of baby spinach or
    4 silverbeet leaves, trimmed
      and well washed
60 g (2 oz) chinese rice stick noodles
extra oil
16 large basil leaves, fried until crisp
extra coriander for garnish
serves 4–6

1 In a large saucepan, heat the oil and sauté the spring onions briefly. Add the button mushrooms and sauté. Add the coriander, fish sauce and lime juice and cook for 2 more minutes, until most of the liquid has evaporated. Add the rice and stir to coat. Add the white wine and allow the liquid to absorb while stirring.

2 In a separate pan, heat the stock and keep at simmering point. Add half a cup (125 ml, 4 fl oz) stock at a time to the saucepan, stirring well after each addition and allowing all liquid to be absorbed before adding the next amount. When half the liquid has been absorbed, add the oyster mushrooms and tuna and stir well. Continue adding stock as usual. When adding the last quantity of stock, add the spinach and stir well. Remove pan from the heat.

3 Heat oil in a clean pan. Crush the noodles with your hands and drop into the hot oil. Allow to sizzle about 30 seconds until golden. Fry basil leaves in pan until crisp.

4 Serve the risotto in individual bowls, garnished with deep-fried crispy noodles, coriander and basil leaves.

preparation time
20 minutes

cooking time
30 minutes

nutritional value per serve
fat: 3.6 g
carbohydrate: 12 g
protein: 5.8 g

risotto niçoise

ingredients

½ cup (125 ml, 4 fl oz) light fish stock
500 g (1 lb) tuna steaks
2 teaspoons olive oil
4 cloves garlic, finely chopped
1 brown onion, chopped
400 g (13 oz) arborio rice
150 ml (5 fl oz) white wine
2 pontiac potatoes, peeled and diced
800 ml (1⅓ pints) vegetable or fish stock, simmering
200 g (7 oz) green beans, trimmed
extra 2 tablespoons stock
1 tablespoon parmesan cheese
90 g (3 oz) pitted kalamata olives, finely chopped
2 handfuls parsley, chopped
serves 4

1 Heat the light fish stock and add the tuna steaks. Poach gently for 5 minutes then remove the fish from the liquid and dice. Reserve the fish liquid.

2 Heat the olive oil and sauté the garlic and onion. Add the rice and stir to coat. Add the wine and allow the liquid to be absorbed. Stir in the potatoes. Begin adding the stock, half a cup (125 ml, 4 fl oz) at a time and stirring well after each addition.

3 When half the stock has been absorbed, add the green beans. Continue adding the stock until all has been absorbed. Add the poaching liquid and diced fish, cover to gently reheat the fish over low heat. Remove the pan from the heat and add the extra stock and parmesan cheese. Toss to combine then remove to a serving platter and garnish with parsley and olives.

i

preparation time
10 minutes

cooking time
25 minutes

nutritional value per serve
fat: 2 g
carbohydrate: 14 g
protein: 7.7 g

fish stuffed with arabic rice

ingredients

1.2-1.5 kg (2¹/₂-3 lb) whole fish, such as
   snapper, bream, sea bass or red
   mullet, cleaned and scaled

arabic rice stuffing

2 teaspoons vegetable oil
1 onion, chopped
¹/₂ cup (100 g, 3¹/₂ oz) brown rice, cooked
2 tablespoons pine nuts
2 tablespoons currants
2 tablespoons chopped fresh parsley
¹/₂ teaspoon ground allspice
2 tablespoons lemon juice
freshly ground black pepper

serves 4

1 To make stuffing, heat oil in a frying pan over a medium heat. Add onion and fry for 4 minutes or until onion is golden. In a bowl, combine onion, rice, pine nuts, currants, parsley, allspice, lemon juice and pepper. Set aside.

2 Wash fish and dry with absorbent paper. Make cavity of fish larger by cutting along the back bone almost to the tail. Fill cavity with stuffing and secure opening with a bamboo skewer.

3 Preheat oven to 180°C (350°F, gas mark 4). Place fish in the centre of a sheet of oiled aluminium foil. Lift edges to enclose fish and seal with a double fold. Place on a baking rack in a baking dish, adding hot water to the dish. Bake in oven for 25 minutes or until flesh flakes when tested.

preparation time
10 minutes

cooking time
25 minutes

nutritional value per serve
fat: 3.1 g
carbohydrate: 5.6 g
protein: 17.7 g

prawn jambalaya

ingredients

3 rashers bacon, cut into strips
1 large onion, finely chopped
1 green capsicum (pepper), diced
1 celery stalk, chopped
3 cloves garlic, crushed
1 cup (200 g, 7 oz) long-grain rice
440 g (14 oz) can tomatoes
2 cups (500 ml, 16 fl oz) chicken stock, boiling
2 teaspoons cajun spice mix
1 teaspoon dried thyme
500 g (1 lb) green medium prawns, shelled and de-veined
155 g (5 oz) smoked ham in one piece, cut into 1 cm cubes
2 spring onions (green onions), finely chopped

serves 4

i

preparation time
20 minutes

cooking time
43 minutes

nutritional value per serve
fat: 0.8 g
carbohydrate: 8.6 g
protein: 7.9 g

1 Cook bacon in a frying pan over a medium heat for 5 minutes or until crisp. Remove bacon from pan and drain on absorbent paper.

2 Add onion to pan and cook, stirring, for 5 minutes or until onion is soft, but not brown. Add capsicum, celery and garlic and cook for 3 minutes. Add rice and cook, stirring frequently, for 5 minutes or until rice becomes translucent. Add the tomatoes and their juices; slash through with a knife to break up. Stir in stock, spice mix and thyme and bring to the boil. Cover, reduce heat to low and cook for 15 minutes.

3 Stir in prawns and ham, cover and cook for a further 10 minutes or until rice is tender and liquid absorbed. Sprinkle with crisp bacon and spring onions and serve immediately.

tomato and tuna risotto

ingredients

2 tablespoons olive oil
2 tablespoons fresh rosemary spikes
$^1/_4$ teaspoon chilli flakes
   or $^1/_2$ teaspoon fresh chilli
4 cloves garlic, crushed
2 onions, sliced thinly
400 g (13 oz) arborio rice
180 ml (6 fl oz) white wine
900 ml (1 $^1/_2$ pints) rich vegetable stock,
   simmering
400 g (13 oz) can tuna, flaked
1 tablespoon tomato paste
2 tablespoons sun-dried tomatoes,
   chopped
400 g (13 oz) can tomatoes
2 handfuls parsley, chopped
4 tablespoons sour cream or
   mascarpone cheese
2 roma tomatoes, finely diced
4 spring onions (green onions),
   very finely chopped
extra fresh herbs, chopped
freshly ground black pepper
serves 6

1 In a saucepan, heat the olive oil and add the rosemary, chilli, garlic and onion. Cook over a high heat until the vegetables are soft and aromatic. Add the arborio rice and stir well to coat each grain.

2 Add the wine and cook over high heat until the liquid has been absorbed. Add a ladle of simmering stock, the flaked tuna, tomato paste, sun-dried tomatoes, canned tomatoes and parsley. Continue to stir and simmer until all liquid has been absorbed. Add stock ladle by ladle, allowing each to be absorbed before adding the next addition.

3 Remove the pan from the heat and stand covered for 10 minutes then add half the sour cream.

4 Garnish with a dollop of remaining sour cream, roma tomatoes and spring onions. Sprinkle on extra fresh herbs and black pepper.

preparation time
15 minutes

cooking time
25 minutes

**nutritional value
per serve**
fat: 4.2 g
carbohydrate: 20 g
protein: 10.3 g

lobster provençale

ingredients

1¼ cups (250 g, 8 oz) long-grain rice
4 tablespoons butter
1 teaspoon freshly crushed garlic
2 spring onions (green onions), chopped
310 g (10 oz) canned tomatoes, chopped
salt and cracked black peppercorns
pinch of saffron
1 large cooked lobster or 4 cooked lobster tails
4 tablespoons brandy
½ bunch fresh chives, chopped, for garnish
1 lemon

serves 4

i

preparation time
15 minutes

cooking time
15 minutes

nutritional value per serve
fat: 4.2 g
carbohydrate: 20 g
protein: 10.3 g

1 Boil the rice 12–13 minutes or until tender, drain and keep hot. In a shallow frying pan, melt butter over a moderate heat. Add garlic, spring onions, tomatoes, salt, pepper and saffron. Cook about 2 minutes until onions are translucent.

2 Remove meat from lobster and cut into large pieces. Add lobster meat to pan and flame with the brandy. Cook gently until lobster is heated through.

3 On serving plate, place rice and sprinkle with chives. Arrange the lobster on the rice and spoon over the sauce from the pan. Serve with lemon wedges.

seafood paella

ingredients

1 tablespoon olive oil
2 onions, chopped
2 cloves garlic, crushed
375 g (12 oz) long-grain white rice
1 litre (1²/₃ pints) chicken stock
pinch saffron threads
250 g (8 oz) calamari (squid) rings
185 g (6 oz) smoked ham, sliced
250 g (8 oz) chorizo sausage, sliced
440 g (14 oz) can peeled tomatoes,
    undrained and mashed
315 g (10 oz) white fish fillets, cubed
250 g (8 oz) green medium-sized
    prawns, shelled and de-veined
500 g (1 lb) mussels, scrubbed and
    beards removed
125 g (4 oz) peas
serves 6

1 In a paella pan or large deep-frying pan, heat oil over a medium heat. Add onions and garlic and cook, stirring, for 3 minutes, until onions are soft. Add rice and cook, stirring, for 4–5 minutes until rice is translucent.

2 Stir stock, saffron, calamari, ham, sausage and tomatoes into pan and bring to the boil. Reduce heat and simmer, stirring occasionally, for 25 minutes or until rice is tender and liquid is absorbed.

3 Place fish, prawns, mussels and peas on top of rice mixture, add a little extra hot stock or water if needed. Reduce heat to low, cover and cook for 10 minutes or until seafood and peas are cooked. Discard any mussels that do not open after 5 minutes. Serve immediately.

preparation time
15 minutes

cooking time
45 minutes

nutritional value per serve
fat: 3.1 g
carbohydrate: 9.4 g
protein: 8.3 g

crab casserole

ingredients

15 g (½ oz) butter
1 onion, chopped
1 green capsicum (pepper), diced
400 g (13 oz) crabmeat
255 g (8 oz) cooked rice
200 ml (7 fl oz) mayonnaise
4 hard boiled eggs, chopped
100 g (3½ oz) fresh bread, cut in cubes
1 tablespoon parsley flakes
4 tablespoons butter, melted
serves 4

preparation time
10 minutes

cooking time
30 minutes

**nutritional value
per serve**
fat: 11.3 g
carbohydrate: 19 g
protein: 7.5 g

1 Heat butter in small frying pan, add onion and capsicum and stir over a moderate heat until onions are soft. Set aside.

2 Flake the crabmeat. In a heatproof dish, combine crabmeat, cooked rice, mayonnaise and eggs. Add the onion and capsicum.

3 Preheat oven to 180°C (350°F, gas mark 4). Mix together bread cubes, parsley and melted butter and sprinkle over crab mixture. Bake in oven for 20–25 minutes.

nasi goreng

preparation time
10 minutes

cooking time
15-20 minutes

nutritional value per serve
fat: 6.5 g
carbohydrate: 20 g
protein: 11.7 g

ingredients

250 g (8 oz) long-grain rice
1 litre (1²/₃ pints) boiling water
1 teaspoon ground turmeric
3 tablespoons vegetable oil
1 bunch spring onions (green onions),
 thinly sliced
2.5 cm fresh root ginger, finely chopped
1-2 red chillies, deseeded and
 thinly sliced
225 g (7½ oz) pork fillet, thinly sliced
2 cloves garlic, crushed
3 tablespoons soy sauce, or to taste
200 g (7 oz) cooked peeled prawns,
 defrosted if frozen and
 thoroughly dried
juice of ½ lemon
coriander for garnish
serves 4

1 Cook the rice in boiling salted water, with turmeric added, for 12–15 minutes. Drain, then spread on to a large flat baking tray. Leave to cool for 1 hour or until completely cold, fluffing up occasionally with a fork.

2 Heat 2 tablespoons of the oil in a wok or heavy-based frying pan. Add half the spring onions, the ginger and chillies and stir-fry over a low heat for 2–3 minutes until softened. Add the remaining oil and

increase the heat to high. Add the pork and garlic and stir-fry for 3 minutes.

3 Add the rice in 3 batches, stirring after each addition to mix well with the other

ingredients. Add the soy sauce and prawns and stir-fry for 2–3 minutes until hot. Transfer to a bowl and mix in the lemon juice. Sprinkle with the remaining spring onions and garnish with coriander.

meat
and
poultry

thai fried rice

ingredients

2 teaspoons vegetable oil
1 teaspoon red curry paste
2 stalks fresh lemon grass, chopped or
  1 teaspoon dried lemon grass or
    1 teaspoon finely grated lemon
      rind (zest)
2 tablespoons chopped fresh coriander
2 boneless chicken breast fillets, sliced
185 g (6 oz) snow peas (mangetout)
1 red capsicum (pepper), chopped
1 small eggplant (aubergine), chopped
315 g (10 oz) jasmine or basmati rice,
  cooked
3 tablespoons sweet chilli sauce
2 tablespoons sweet soy sauce

serves 4

i

preparation time
10 minutes

cooking time
12 minutes

**nutritional value
per serve**
fat: 3.2 g
carbohydrate: 17 g
protein: 11 g

1 Heat oil in a wok or large frying pan over a high heat. Add curry paste, lemon grass or lemon zest and coriander and stir-fry for 1 minute. Add chicken to pan and stir-fry for 5 minutes or until chicken is just cooked.

2 Add snow peas, capsicum and eggplant and stir-fry for 3 minutes longer. Add rice, chilli sauce and soy sauce. Toss to combine and stir-fry for 3 minutes or until mixture is heated through.

spanish risotto

ingredients

2 tablespoons olive oil
2 tablespoons mild paprika
$^{1}/_{4}$ teaspoon chilli flakes
1 teaspoon turmeric
1 teaspoon powdered saffron
4 cloves garlic, crushed
2 onions, sliced thinly
2 boneless chicken breast fillets,
   sliced thinly
400 g (13 oz) arborio rice
180 ml (6 oz) white wine
2 tablespoons tomato paste
2 handfuls parsley, chopped
grated rind (zest) and juice of 1 orange
900 ml (1$^{1}/_{2}$ pints) rich vegetable,
   chicken or beef stock, simmering
4 spring onions (green onions),
   very finely chopped
1 tablespoon fresh thyme leaves
freshly ground black pepper
serves 4

preparation time
10 minutes

cooking time
25 minutes

**nutritional value
per serve**
fat: 3.1 g
carbohydrate: 13.4 g
protein: 7.2 g

1 Heat the olive oil in a large saucepan. Add the paprika, chilli, turmeric, saffron and garlic. Cook for 1 minute to release the aroma of the spices. Add the onions and cook until very soft. Add the chicken and cook until it turns white.

2 Stir in the rice and the wine. Stir until wine is absorbed. Add the tomato paste, parsley, orange juice and rind. Add the stock, half a cup (125 ml, 4 fl oz) at a time, stirring constantly until liquid is absorbed before adding the next amount. Continue in this manner until all the stock has been absorbed and the rice is firm but tender. Remove the saucepan from the heat. Add the spring onions, thyme and pepper. Serve immediately.

surf and turf risotto

ingredients

2 tablespoons olive oil
4 cloves garlic
400 g (13 oz) beef fillet (tenderloin)
10 spring onions (green onions), chopped
1 red capsicum (pepper), sliced into strips
400 g (13 oz) arborio rice
145 ml (5 fl oz) dry white wine
900 ml (1½ pints) rich vegetable or
    chicken stock, simmering
2 cooked lobster tails, meat removed
    and cubed
2 onions, sliced and deep-fried until crisp
oil for frying
1 tablespoon grated parmesan cheese
fresh parsley, chopped
1 tablespoon sour cream
serves 4

2 Add the rice and stir to coat. Add the wine and simmer until absorbed. Add the stock, half a cup at a time, stirring well and allowing stock to be absorbed before the next addition.

3 With the last addition of stock, add the lobster meat and gently stir through. Remove from heat and stand covered for 10 minutes to absorb the liquid and plump the rice.

4 Stir through the parmesan cheese, parsley and sour cream. Thinly slice the cooked beef. Serve the risotto in individual bowls, topped with beef slices and garnished with the crispy fried onions. Serve immediately.

i

preparation time
10 minutes

cooking time
30 minutes

**nutritional value
per serve**
fat: 2.9 g
carbohydrate: 13 g
protein: 7.1 g

1 In a heavy-based frying pan heat the olive oil and fry the garlic over moderate heat. Add the beef fillet and cook for 3–4 minutes on all sides. Remove from the pan and keep warm wrapped in foil. To the pan, add the spring onions and capsicum and sauté until softened.

fire and spice risotto

ingredients

800 g (1 lb 10 oz) skirt steak (beef flank)
4 tablespoons olive oil
8 cloves garlic, finely chopped or crushed
3 teaspoons fresh grated ginger
1 bunch of spring onions (green onions), chopped
2 small red chillies, finely chopped
2 teaspoons cumin
2 teaspoons ground coriander
2 teaspoons turmeric
400 g (13 oz) arborio rice
100 ml (3½ fl oz) red wine
100 ml (3½ fl oz) sherry
1 litre (1⅔ pints) beef stock, simmering
2 tomatoes, chopped
2 handfuls parsley, chopped
2 handfuls coriander, chopped
2 tablespoons lime juice
90 ml (3 fl oz) yoghurt
1 onion, finely sliced and deep-fried (optional)
extra chopped parsley
serves 4

1 Cut the skirt steak into 2.5 cm wide strips approximately 6 cm long. Set aside.

2 Heat olive oil in a large heavy-based saucepan. Add garlic, ginger, spring onions and chilli and stir over heat for 4 minutes. Add the beef strips and stir to brown on all sides. Stir in cumin, coriander and turmeric and stir 2 minutes. Add the rice and stir to coat the grains with oil and spices.

3 Add the wine, sherry and half of the hot stock. Bring to the boil while stirring, turn heat down to low, cover and simmer for 12 minutes. Stir in remaining hot stock, tomatoes, parsley and coriander. Cover and simmer for 8 minutes more. Turn off heat and stand covered 5 minutes.

4 Stir in the lime juice. Serve in individual bowls, garnished with a little yoghurt, a mound of fried onion and a sprinkling of parsley.

i

preparation time
10 minutes

cooking time
30 minutes

nutritional value per serve
fat: 3.6 g
carbohydrate: 11.1 g
protein: 6.7 g

lamb fillets with salsa pilaf

ingredients

750 g (1 1/2 lb) lamb fillets
1/2 teaspoon crushed garlic
1 tablespoon lemon juice
2 teaspoons olive oil
salt and pepper
1 1/4 cups (250 g, 8 oz) long-grain rice
1.5 litres (2 1/2 pints) boiling water
60 g (2 oz) pine nuts, toasted
300 g (10 oz) jar tomato salsa
2 tablespoons currants
serves 4–5

preparation time
10 minutes, plus
30 minutes
standing

cooking time
25 minutes

**nutritional value
per serve**
fat: 5.4 g
carbohydrate: 19 g
protein: 12.6 g

1 Trim the lamb fillets, removing the fine silver membrane. Place in a dish and add garlic, lemon juice, oil, salt and pepper. Cover and stand 30 minutes. Cook the rice in salted boiling water for about 15 minutes, until tender. Drain well and keep hot.

2 Heat a small frying pan, add pine nuts and shake over heat until coloured. Add the salsa and currants and heat through.

3 Heat grill plate and oil lightly, set at medium-high. Place lamb on grill and cook 6–8 minutes, turning to cook on all sides. Cook longer for well done. Rest 5 minutes before slicing into 1 cm diagonal cut slices.

4 Using a cup or mould, form a mound of rice on the plate. Pour salsa over the rice and arrange lamb slices at base of rice mould.

persian-style pilaf

ingredients

3 tablespoons olive oil
6 cloves garlic, crushed
2 large brown onions, roughly chopped
600 g (1¼ lb) lamb fillets, sliced
2 teaspoons cumin
400 g (13 oz) arborio rice
1 litre (1⅔ pints) vegetable stock,
    simmering
1 cinnamon stick
5 fresh dates, chopped
100 g (3½ oz) dried apricots, whole
10 prunes, whole
200 g (7 oz) walnuts, toasted and
    cut in half
2 tablespoons chopped coriander
2 tablespoons thick yoghurt
100 g (3½ oz) pistachio nuts,
    roughly chopped

serves 4-6

1 Heat the oil in a large saucepan. Add the garlic and onion and fry gently until onion is soft. Add the lamb and stir over high heat to brown, stir in the cumin.

2 Add the rice and quickly stir to coat the grains then stir in half of the hot stock. Add the cinnamon stick, turn heat down, cover and simmer 12 minutes or until liquid has just absorbed.

3 Add remaining hot stock, dates, apricots, prunes and walnuts. Cover and simmer 8 minutes or until rice is still a little firm. Turn off heat and stand covered for 5–8 minutes until liquid is absorbed. Remove the cinnamon stick, fluff the rice with a fork and stir in coriander.

4 Serve in individual warm bowls. Place a dollop of yoghurt on top and sprinkle with the pistachio nuts.

preparation time
15 minutes

cooking time
25 minutes, plus 5
minutes standing

**nutritional value
per serve**
fat: 8.9 g
carbohydrate: 15.1 g
protein: 7.3 g

malay beef risotto

ingredients

2 tablespoons sesame or peanut oil
6 spring onions (green onions),
  finely chopped
4 cloves garlic, crushed
1 teaspoon cumin
$1/2$-1 teaspoon red chilli, finely chopped
500 g (1 lb) lean beef, cubed
1 litre (1 $2/3$ pints) hot beef or
  vegetable stock
400 g (13 oz) long-grain rice
100 ml (3 $1/2$ fl oz) rice wine
6 tablespoons chunky peanut butter
2 tablespoons soy sauce
$1/2$ chinese cabbage, finely shredded
1 tablespoon lime juice
90 g (3 oz) roasted peanuts, chopped
serves 4-6

1 Heat the sesame or peanut oil in a large heavy-based saucepan. Add the spring onions, garlic, cumin and chilli. Sauté for 2 minutes, add the beef cubes and sauté for about 5 minutes until browned. Add 1 cup of stock, turn down heat and simmer for 15 minutes.

2 Add the rice, the rice wine, peanut butter, soy sauce

and the remaining stock. Bring to the boil, add the shredded cabbage, reduce heat, cover and simmer for 15 minutes. Turn off heat and stand covered for 5 minutes before serving.

3 Pile the risotto into individual bowls, sprinkle with lime juice and chopped roasted peanuts.

barbecued chicken gado

ingredients

500 g (1 lb) chicken tenderloins
1 cup (250 ml, 8 fl oz) satay marinade
1½ cups (330 g, 11 oz) short-grain rice
200 g (7 oz) green beans, halved
60 g (2 oz) roasted unsalted peanuts

satay marinade

125 g (4 oz) peanut butter
½ teaspoon chilli powder
½ teaspoon ground ginger
2 tablespoons lemon juice
1 tablespoon brown sugar
½ cup (125 ml, 4 fl oz) coconut milk

serves 5

1 In a small saucepan, place all marinade ingredients, heat and stir to combine. Place chicken in a non-metal dish and add enough marinade to coat well, reserving the remainder. Cover and stand for 30 minutes, or longer in refrigerator.

2 Cook rice in boiling, salted water for about 15 minutes until tender. Drain well. Boil beans until tender but still crisp, drain. Mix rice, beans and half the roasted peanuts together. Keep hot.

3 Place a sheet of silicon baking paper on top of hot barbecue grill bars and place the tenderloins on the paper. Cook for 2 minutes on each side on high heat, brushing with marinade during cooking. Heat reserved marinade, on barbecue.

4 Pile rice into centre of heated plates. Arrange 2–3 tenderloins over the rice, top with heated satay marinade and sprinkle with remaining roasted peanuts.

i

preparation time
10 minutes, plus 30 minutes marinating

cooking time
20 minutes

nutritional value
fat: 13.7 g
carbohydrate: 21 g
protein: 12.3 g

risotto with veal and sage

ingredients

2 tablespoons butter or olive oil
350 g (11^1/$_2$ oz) veal, cut into cubes
2 tablespoons tomato paste
30 g (1 oz) fresh sage leaves, chopped
2 tablespoons chopped parsley
^{3}/$_4$ cup (185 ml, 6 fl oz) beef or veal stock
extra 2 tablespoons olive oil
2 cloves garlic, crushed
1 medium leek, thinly sliced
2 cups (440 g, 14 oz) arborio rice
200 ml (7 fl oz) red wine such as chianti
1.5 litres (2^1/$_2$ pints) beef or veal stock,
  boiling
2 handfuls chopped flat-leaf parsley
60 g (2 oz) parmesan cheese, grated
1 bunch sage leaves, crispy fried to
  garnish
serves 4

1 In a sauté pan, heat the olive oil or butter until very hot and add the veal. Cook quickly until the meat changes colour. Add the tomato paste, sage, parsley and ^{3}/$_4$ cup (185 ml, 6 fl oz) stock. Simmer for 20 minutes until the meat is tender.

2 In a separate pot, heat the extra 2 tablespoons olive oil. Add the garlic and leek and sauté until the vegetables are softened. Add the rice and stir to coat. Add the wine and stir until evaporated.

3 Begin to add the simmering stock one ladle at a time, allowing each ladle of stock to be absorbed before the next one is added. Continue adding stock in the same fashion until it has all been used. Remove from heat and add parmesan cheese, extra parsley and veal mixture. Serve immediately over a small pile of crispy sage leaves.

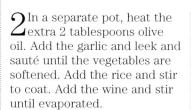

preparation time
15 minutes

cooking time
30 minutes

**nutritional value
per serve**
fat: 3.4 g
carbohydrate: 11 g
protein: 0.8 g

rice with chicken livers, pine nuts and currants

ingredients

500 g (1 lb) chicken livers
75 g (2½ oz) butter
12 spring onions (green onions), chopped
1½ cups (330 g, 11 oz) short-grain rice
750 ml (1¼ pints) chicken stock
2 handfuls parsley, chopped
100 g (3½ oz) pine nuts
100 g (3½ oz) currants

serves 8

i

preparation time
10 minutes

cooking time
35 minutes, plus
10 minutes
standing

**nutritional value
per serve**
fat: 7.6 g
carbohydrate: 16.2 g
protein: 6.7 g

1 Wash chicken livers, and remove any sinew. Chop livers in half.

2 Heat butter in a large saucepan and sauté the spring onions for 5 minutes until tender. Add the chicken livers and sauté for a few minutes until they change colour.

3 Add the rice and chicken stock to the saucepan and bring to the boil. Simmer with the lid on, stirring occasionally, for approximately 25 minutes. Add the parsley, pine nuts and currants, stir through the rice, and cook a further 3 minutes. Turn off heat and stand covered for 10 minutes.

apricot chicken pilaf

ingredients

1½ cups (300 g, 10oz) long-grain rice
  water for soaking
1 teaspoon salt
1 kg (2 lb) chicken thigh fillets
3 tablespoons butter
1 large onion, finely chopped
45 g (1½ oz) pine nuts
½ teaspoon fresh thyme, chopped
salt and freshly ground black pepper
¼ teaspoon ground cinnamon
3½ cups (875 ml, 28 fl oz) hot
  chicken stock
100 g (3½ oz) diced dried apricots
100 g (3½ oz) seeded raisins
serves 6

i

preparation time
10 minutes, plus 2
hours soaking

cooking time
45-50 minutes

**nutritional value
per serve**
fat: 5.9 g
carbohydrate: 13 g
protein: 3.7 g

1 Place rice in water to cover, add salt and soak for 2 hours. Drain thoroughly. Cut each thigh fillet into 3 or 4 pieces. Heat 2 tablespoons butter in a large, heavy-based saucepan and brown the chicken well on all sides over high heat. Remove to a plate.

2 Add remaining butter and sauté the onion and pine nuts. Add thyme, salt, pepper and cinnamon. Add the drained rice and stir to coat well with butter. Heat chicken stock to boiling and pour over the rice. Return chicken pieces to saucepan and stir in apricots and raisins. Bring back to the boil for 2 minutes, then lower the heat, cover the saucepan and simmer for 10 minutes.

3 Place a folded tea towel under the saucepan lid, pressing lid down tightly. Turn down heat to very low and cook for 30–35 minutes undisturbed. Fluff up rice with a fork and serve hot.

vegetables

risotto of tomato and basil

ingredients

1 tablespoon butter
1 tablespoon olive oil
2 cloves garlic, minced
1 onion, finely chopped
400 g (13 oz) arborio rice
½ cup (125 ml, 4 fl oz) dry white wine
1 litre (1⅔ pints) vegetable or chicken
  stock, simmering
4 roma tomatoes, halved lengthwise
8 sun-dried tomatoes, chopped
20 fresh basil leaves, cut into strips
30 g (1 oz) parmesan cheese, grated
2 tablespoons mascarpone cheese
salt and freshly ground black pepper
extra basil leaves for garnish
serves 4-6

1 Heat the butter and oil in a large saucepan. Add the garlic and onion and sauté until the onion is transparent. Add the rice and stir to coat. Add the wine and stir until absorbed.

i

preparation time
5 minutes

cooking time
30 minutes

nutritional value per serve
fat: 3.2 g
carbohydrate: 15 g
protein: 2.6 g

2 Add half the stock a ladle at a time, stirring each addition until absorbed before adding the next ladle of stock.

3 Add the roma tomatoes, sun-dried tomatoes and basil, and stir well. Continue to add stock until the rice is still firm to bite and all the liquid has been absorbed.

4 Remove the saucepan from the heat and stir through the parmesan, mascarpone, salt and pepper. Garnish with extra basil leaves and serve immediately.

mushroom and black olive risotto

ingredients

15 g (¹/₂ oz) dried porcini mushrooms
200 ml (7 fl oz) boiling water
3 tablespoons olive oil
1 onion, chopped
250 g (8 oz) large field (open)
 mushrooms, chopped
250 g (8 oz) arborio rice
2 tablespoons pitted black olives,
 roughly chopped
450 ml (14 fl oz) vegetable stock
salt and black pepper
2 tablespoons black olive paste
60 g (2 oz) parmesan cheese
 cut from a block
serves 4

i

preparation time
10 minutes, plus
20 minutes
soaking

cooking time
30 minutes, plus
5 minutes
standing

**nutritional value
per serve**
fat: 6.4 g
carbohydrate: 17 g
protein: 4.5 g

1 Cover the porcini with boiling water and leave to soak for 20 minutes. Drain, reserving the water, and set aside. Heat the oil in a large heavy-based saucepan. Add the onion and field mushrooms and fry for 4–5 minutes. Add the rice and stir to coat with the oil. Fry for 1–2 minutes.

2 Add the porcini and the reserved liquid to the rice with the olives and half the vegetable stock. Cover and simmer for 10 minutes or until the liquid has been absorbed, stirring occasionally.

3 Stir in 100 ml (3¹/₂ fl oz) of the remaining stock and cook for 5 minutes, covered, until absorbed. Add the remaining stock, salt, pepper and olive paste and cook for 5 minutes, uncovered, stirring constantly. Remove from the heat and stand, covered, for 5 minutes. Transfer to a serving dish. Shave over the parmesan, using a vegetable peeler, and serve.

cheesy baked rice

ingredients

2 tablespoons butter or margarine
2 leeks, sliced
3 rashers bacon, chopped
1/2 red capsicum (pepper),
  finely chopped
60 g (2 oz) long-grain rice, cooked
1 1/2 cups (375 ml, 12 fl oz) milk
2 eggs, lightly beaten
1/2 teaspoon dry mustard
1 teaspoon worcestershire sauce
1 tablespoon mayonnaise
125 g (4 oz) mild cheddar, grated
2 tablespoons chopped fresh parsley
freshly ground black pepper
1 teaspoon paprika

serves 4

i

preparation time
10 minutes

cooking time
40 minutes

**nutritional value
per serve**
fat: 11.1 g
carbohydrate: 7.7 g
protein: 8.9 g

1 Preheat oven to 180°C (350°F, gas mark 4). Melt butter or margarine in a frying pan over a medium heat. Add leeks, bacon and capsicum and cook, stirring, for 4–5 minutes or until leeks are soft and bacon is brown. Mix with the rice and spoon mixture into a

lightly greased ovenproof dish, set aside.

2 Heat milk to hot but not boiling. In a bowl, whisk together the eggs, mustard, worcestershire sauce, mayonnaise, cheddar, parsley and black pepper.

3 Gradually whisk a few spoonfuls of hot milk into the egg mixture to temper the egg. Slowly pour in the remaining milk, while stirring.

4 Carefully pour the combined milk egg mixture into the ovenproof dish containing the rice and leeks.

5 Place dish in a baking dish with enough hot water to come halfway up the sides. Bake in oven for 28–30 minutes or until custard is firm.

risotto mexicana

ingredients

2 tablespoons olive oil
1 teaspoon finely chopped red chilli
2 cloves garlic, finely chopped
2 onions, sliced
400 g (13 oz) arborio rice
1/2 butternut pumpkin, cut into chunks
1 litre (1²/₃ pints) rich vegetable stock, simmering
1 celery stalk, chopped
2 tomatoes, chopped
100 ml (3¹/₂ fl oz) taco sauce
1 red capsicum (pepper), chopped roughly
6 spring onions (green onions), chopped
100 g (3¹/₂ oz) flaked almonds, toasted
100 g (3¹/₂ oz) sultanas or raisins
60 g (2 oz) pumpkin seeds (pepitas)
extra 2 tablespoons taco sauce
(optional)
serves 4-6

i

preparation time
10 minutes

cooking time
25 minutes, plus
5-10 minutes
standing

nutritional value per serve
fat: 4.7 g
carbohydrate: 16 g
protein: 3.2 g

1 Heat the olive oil in a large saucepan. Add the chilli, garlic and onions. Sauté for 5 minutes or until softened. Add the rice and stir 1 minute. Add the pumpkin and stir.

2 Add half of the stock and stir well. Simmer covered for 12 minutes until the liquid has been absorbed. Add the celery and tomatoes, remaining stock and taco sauce. Cover and simmer 8 minutes more.

3 Remove the pan from the heat and quickly add the capsicum, spring onions, flaked almonds and sultanas or raisins. Cover and stand 5–10 minutes before serving. Fluff up with a fork tossing in the pumpkin seeds. Transfer to a serving dish and serve immediately. Drizzle with extra taco sauce if desired.

sticky rice with beansprouts

ingredients

250 g (8 oz) glutinous rice
water
pinch salt
225 g (7½ oz) beansprouts or
   mung dhal
serves 4

1 Cover rice with salted water and leave to soak overnight. Wash rice until water runs clear and drain.

2 Line a bamboo steamer or top of a metal steamer with a tea towel and spread rice over it. Cover with folded sides of tea towel and/or lid. Steam on top of a wok or saucepan of boiling water for about 40 minutes, replenishing water until cooked. Add beansprouts to cooked rice and fluff through with a fork. Serve to accompany asian dishes.

i

preparation time
5 minutes, plus
overnight soaking

preparation time
40 minutes

**nutritional value
per serve**
fat: 0.2 g
carbohydrate: 15 g
protein: 2.7 g

risotto with baby spinach and gorgonzola

ingredients

1 litre (1 2/3 pints) chicken stock
2 tablespoons olive oil
2 cloves garlic, crushed
1 onion, finely chopped
2 cups (440 g, 14 oz) arborio rice
125 ml (4 fl oz) white wine
225 g (7 1/2 oz) baby spinach
225 g (7 1/2 oz) gorgonzola cheese, in small pieces
salt and freshly ground pepper
serves 6

i

preparation time
10 minutes

cooking time
25 minutes

nutritional value per serve
fat: 5.4 g
carbohydrate: 16 g
protein: 4.2 g

1 In a saucepan, place stock and bring to the boil. Leave simmering. Heat oil in a large saucepan. Add garlic and onion, and cook for 5 minutes until soft. Add rice and stir until well coated. Pour in wine and cook until the liquid has been absorbed.

2 Add the stock to the saucepan, a ladle at a time, stirring continuously until liquid has been absorbed before adding the next ladle of stock. Keep adding stock this way, and stirring, until all the stock is used and the rice is cooked, but still a little firm to bite.

3 Add the spinach, gorgonzola, salt and pepper. Stir and cook until spinach is just wilted and cheese has melted. Serve immediately.

risotto of chinese aromatics

ingredients

15 g (¹/₂ oz) black cloud fungus or
    chinese dried mushrooms
1 cup (250 ml, 8 fl oz) boiling water
1 tablespoon olive oil
1 tablespoon toasted sesame oil
1 bunch spring onions (green onions)
2 cloves garlic, crushed
1-2 tablespoons grated fresh ginger
¹/₂ teaspoon chopped fresh red chillies
400 g (13 oz) arborio rice
200 ml (7 fl oz) dry white wine
2 tablespoons soy sauce, or to taste
1 tablespoon fish sauce
1 tablespoon black bean sauce
800 ml (1¹/₃ pints) vegetable stock,
    simmering
45 g (1¹/₂ oz) bean shoots
2 handfuls fresh mint, chopped
2 handfuls fresh coriander, chopped
extra 2 tablespoons fresh coriander
150 g (5 oz) piece tofu, diced
extra 2 teaspoons toasted sesame oil
serves 4-6

2 In a saucepan, add the oils, spring onions, garlic, ginger and red chillies. Sauté for 3 minutes. Add the rice and stir to coat. Add the wine, soy sauce, fish sauce, black bean sauce and black cloud fungus and stir until absorbed.

3 Add the reserved soaking liquid to the simmering stock. Begin adding the stock to the saucepan, half a cup at a time, stirring well after each addition. Add the bean shoots, coriander and mint, with the last cup of stock.

4 When most of the stock has been absorbed, remove the pan from the heat and stand covered for 5 minutes. Garnish with the tofu cubes, fresh coriander and a drizzle of sesame oil. Serve immediately.

1 Rinse the black cloud fungus well. Soak in boiling hot water for 30 minutes. Drain and reserve the soaking liquid.

preparation time
10 minutes, plus
30 minutes
soaking

cooking time
25 minutes

**nutritional value
per serve**
fat: 3.2 g
carbohydrate: 17 g
protein: 3.3 g

green rice with herbs

ingredients

2 teaspoons oil
1 onion, quartered and roasted
2 cloves garlic, unpeeled and roasted
8 spinach or rocket leaves
3 tablespoons chopped flat-leaf parsley
3 tablespoons chopped fresh coriander
2 mild green chillies, deseeded
  and chopped
3 cups (750 ml, 1 1/4 pints) hot
  chicken stock
1 tablespoon vegetable oil
1 cup (220 g, 7 1/2 oz) white
  short-grain rice

serves 6

i

preparation time
5 minutes

cooking time
40 minutes

**nutritional value
per serve**
fat: 2.8 g
carbohydrate: 15 g
protein: 2.2 g

1 Heat a small frying pan. Add 2 teaspoons oil, the quartered onion and unpeeled garlic. Turn to coat with oil. Reduce heat to low, cover and cook for 10 minutes, turning after 5 minutes. Remove and peel the garlic. In a food processor or blender, place onion, garlic, spinach, parsley, coriander, chillies and 1/3 cup (90 ml, 3 fl oz) stock and process to make a purée.

2 Heat oil in a separate saucepan over a medium heat. Add rice and cook stirring for 2–3 minutes or until rice is opaque. Stir in herb purée and remaining hot stock. Bring to simmering, cover and simmer for 20–25 minutes or until rice is tender and liquid absorbed. Fluff up with a fork and serve immediately.

indonesian rice

ingredients

1½ cups (300 g, 10 oz) basmati rice
2 tablespoons vegetable oil
2 onions, sliced
2 cloves garlic, crushed
2 teaspoons ground cumin
1 teaspoon ground coriander
2 teaspoons ground cardamom
2 fresh red chillies, chopped
2½ cups (625 ml, 1 pint) chicken stock
2 tablespoons honey
1 tablespoon soy sauce
2 spring onions (scallions, green onions), chopped

serves 4

1 Place rice in a bowl, pour over enough hot water to cover and set aside to stand for 3 minutes. Drain.

2 Heat oil in a large frying pan. Add onions and garlic and stir-fry for 4–5 minutes or until onion is soft. Add cumin, coriander, cardamom, chillies and rice and stir-fry for 1 minute. In a bowl, combine stock, honey and soy sauce. Stir into rice mixture and bring to the boil. Reduce heat and boil gently for 10 minutes.

3 Turn heat to very low, cover and cook for 5 minutes longer. Remove from heat, stand covered 5–10 minutes to absorb remaining liquid. Stir in spring onions and serve immediately.

i

preparation tme
8 minutes

cooking time
25 minutes, plus 10 minutes standing

nutritional value
fat: 3.2 g
carbohydrate: 23.9 g
protein: 2.5 g

chilli fried rice

ingredients

2 teaspoons vegetable oil
2 fresh red chillies, chopped
1 tablespoon thai red curry paste
2 onions, sliced
1¹/₂ cups (330 g, 11 oz) short-grain rice, cooked and cooled
125 g (4 oz) snake (yard-long) or green beans, chopped into 1.5 cm pieces
125 g (4 oz) baby bok choy (pak choi), blanched
3 tablespoons lime juice
2 teaspoons thai fish sauce

serves 4

i

preparation time
20 minutes
including
cooked rice

cooking time
8 minutes

nutritional value per serve
fat: 2.5 g
carbohydrate: 11.7 g
protein: 1.9 g

1 Heat oil in a wok or frying pan over a high heat. Add chillies and curry paste and stir-fry for 1 minute or until fragrant. Add onions and stir-fry for 3 minutes or until soft.

2 Add rice, beans and bok choy to pan and stir-fry for 4 minutes or until rice is heated through. Stir in lime juice and fish sauce.

fragrant pilaf

ingredients

large pinch of saffron strands
1 tablespoon boiling water
2 tablespoons butter
1 golden shallot, finely chopped
3 cardamom pods
1 cinnamon stick
1¼ cups (250 g, 8 oz) basmati rice,
   rinsed and drained
400 ml (13 fl oz) hot water
pinch salt
serves 4

preparation time
5 minutes

cooking time
20 minutes

nutritional value
fat: 0.1 g
carbohydrate: 26 g
protein: 0.1 g

1 Soak the saffron strands with 1 tablespoon water and set aside. Melt the butter in a large, heavy-based saucepan. Fry the shallot gently for 2 minutes or until softened. Add the cardamom pods, cinnamon and rice and mix well.

2 Add the hot water, salt and strain in the saffron liquid. Bring to the boil, then reduce the heat and cover the pan tightly. Simmer for 15 minutes or until the liquid has been absorbed and the rice is tender. Remove the cardamom pods and cinnamon stick before serving. Serve to accompany grilled fish or chicken.

summer rice salad with sweet chilli dressing

ingredients

2 cups (400 g, 13 oz) long-grain rice, cooked and cooled

440 g (14 oz) can chickpeas, rinsed and drained

4 spring onions (green onions), chopped

1 red capsicum (pepper), sliced

2 tablespoons chopped fresh mint

1 small pineapple, diced

2 mangoes, peeled and sliced

60 g (2 oz) flaked almonds, toasted

dressing

2 tablespoons sweet chilli sauce

1 tablespoon lemon or lime juice

1/2 teaspoon soy sauce

serves 6

i

preparation time
15 minutes

cooking time
15 minutes

nutritional value
fat: 2.7 g
carbohydrate: 14.1 g
protein: 3 g

1 In a large salad bowl, mix the rice and chickpeas.

2 Add the spring onions, capsicum and mint and toss. Add the pineapple, mango and half of the flaked almonds.

3 In a small bowl, combine the sweet chilli sauce, lemon or lime juice and soy sauce. Toss carefully through the salad. Sprinkle over remaining almonds.

fried brown rice

ingredients

1½ cups (330 g, 11 oz) brown rice
2 tablespoons peanut oil
2 eggs, lightly beaten
2 celery stalks, chopped
1 red capsicum (pepper), chopped
2 cloves garlic, crushed
90 g (3 oz) frozen peas, cooked and drained
4 spring onions (green onions), chopped
1 tablespoon soy sauce
serves 4–6

i

preparation time
10 minutes

cooking time
40 minutes,
plus 3 hours
refrigeration

**nutritional value
per serve**
fat: 7 g
carbohydrate: 31 g
protein: 5.8 g

1 Cook rice in boiling water for about 30 minutes until tender. Drain well, spread out on a tray and refrigerate uncovered for 2 hours to dry out. Toss and re-spread after 1 hour.

2 Heat 2 teaspoons oil in a wok or small frying pan, swirl to coat the base. Pour eggs into pan and cook over a low heat, tilting the wok or pan to spread the egg. Cook until eggs are set. Tip out the omelette and slice thinly.

3 Heat remaining oil in the wok or large frying pan, add celery, capsicum and garlic and stir-fry for 3–4 minutes. Add the rice and peas and stir-fry 2 minutes to heat well. Add the egg strips, spring onions and soy sauce and toss to distribute. Serve immediately.

desserts

sticky rice and mango

ingredients

2 cups (440 g, 14 oz) short-grain white
   glutinous rice, soaked overnight
1 cup (250 ml, 8 fl oz) coconut milk
3 tablespoons sugar
6 tablespoons very thick coconut cream
2 mangoes, peeled and sliced
serves 6

1 Drain the soaked rice in a colander and rinse under cold running water until water runs clear. Place in a saucepan and pour enough cold water to cover. Cover pan with a tight-fitting lid and cook over a low heat for 15–20 minutes or until water is absorbed.

2 Place rice in a shallow dish. Combine coconut milk and sugar and quickly stir into rice. Cover tightly with plastic cling wrap and stand for 25 minutes. The retained heat will absorb the coconut milk.

3 Spoon rice into serving dishes, top with 1 tablespoon thick coconut cream and serve with sliced mangoes.

i

preparation time
5 minutes, plus
overnight soaking

cooking time
20 minutes, plus
25 minutes
standing

**nutritional value
per serve**
fat: 6.4 g
carbohydrate: 35 g
protein: 3.1 g

citrus risotto

ingredients

2 oranges
2 tablespoons butter
4 tablespoons sugar
rind (zest) of 1 lime, grated
rind of 1 lemon, grated
rind of 1 orange, grated
400 g (13 oz) arborio rice
100 ml (3½ fl oz) white wine
800 ml (1⅓ pints) orange juice,
   simmering
juice of 1 lemon
juice of 1 lime
2 tablespoons demerara sugar
60 g (2 oz) flaked almonds, toasted
serves 4

1 To segment the orange, peel thickly cutting away all the pith. Cut out the segments on either side of the membrane.

i

preparation time
10 minutes

cooking time
25 minutes

**nutritional value
per serve**
fat: 3.7 g
carbohydrate: 28 g
protein: 2.5 g

2 In a saucepan, place the butter, sugar and grated rind. Stir well over moderate heat to melt the butter. Add the rice and stir to coat the grains for 1 minute. Add the white wine and stir until the liquid is absorbed. Add 1 cup of orange juice and stir until absorbed. Continue in this fashion until all the juice has been added and absorbed and the rice is tender. This process will take about 25 minutes.

3 Stir through the orange segments, lemon juice, lime juice and sugar. Place into serving bowls. Garnish with toasted almonds.

champagne and strawberry risotto

ingredients

600 ml (1 pint) water
150 g (5 oz) sugar
2 tablespoons butter
200 g (7 oz) strawberries, chopped
400 g (13 oz) arborio rice
400 ml (13 fl oz) champagne
200 g (7 oz) strawberries, whole
2 tablespoons bottled strawberry syrup
6 savionie biscuits

serves 6

1 Mix the water and sugar together in a small saucepan and bring to the boil, turn down to a slow simmer. Simmer gently while you begin the risotto.

2 Heat the butter and sauté the chopped strawberries until softened. Add the rice and stir to coat, cooking for a moment or two until the butter has been absorbed by the rice. Add the champagne and simmer until the rice has absorbed the liquid.

3 Add the sugar syrup, 1 cup (250 ml, 8 fl oz) at a time, stirring well after each addition and allowing the liquid to be absorbed before the next addition.

4 When all the sugar syrup has been absorbed, remove the pan from the heat. Stir in remaining strawberries and strawberry syrup. Serve immediately over savionie biscuits, with a little extra syrup spooned over the top.

i

preparation time
5 minutes

cooking time
25 minutes

nutritional value per serve
fat: 2.5 g
carbohydrate: 36 g
protein: 2.7 g

risotto of caramelised apples and pears

ingredients

3 tablespoons butter
3 tablespoons sugar
2 tablespoons maple syrup
2 golden delicious apples, peeled, cored and sliced
1 brown pear, peeled, cored and sliced
1 teaspoon cinnamon
600 ml (1 pint) apple juice
300 ml (10 fl oz) water
1 tablespoon butter
400 g (13 oz) arborio rice
100 ml (3½ fl oz) white wine
4 tablespoons sour cream
½ teaspoon cinnamon
1 red apple, coarse grated and tossed with lemon juice

serves 4-6

1 In a non-stick frying pan, heat the butter, sugar and maple syrup. Boil about 3 minutes until syrupy. Add the sliced fruit and cinnamon, and toss. Simmer the fruit about 10–15 minutes until caramelised and golden. Set aside.

2 In a pan, combine apple juice and water and heat to simmering. In a saucepan, melt the butter, add the rice and stir to coat. Add the wine and simmer until the liquid is absorbed. Begin to add the simmering apple water, 1 cup (250 ml, 8 fl oz) at a time, stirring well after each addition and allowing the liquid to be absorbed before the next addition.

3 When half the apple water has been absorbed, add the caramelised apples and pears and stir well to distribute. Continue adding the apple water as before until it has all been absorbed.

4 Remove the pan from the heat and add half the sour cream. Stir well to distribute and allow to cool. Serve in individual bowls, garnished with a small dollop of sour cream, a sprinkling of cinnamon and some grated apple.

i

preparation time
10 minutes

cooking time
35 minutes

nutritional value
fat: 4.1 g
carbohydrate: 40 g
protein: 1.5 g

fig and rhubarb risotto

ingredients

400 ml (13 fl oz) orange juice
600 ml (1 pint) water
8 ribs (sticks) rhubarb, red part only
2 tablespoons butter
10 dried figs, halved
400 g (13 oz) arborio rice
150 g (5 oz) sugar
1 tablespoon mascarpone cheese
4-6 fresh figs
1 tablespoon brown sugar
serves 6-8

1 In a large pan, heat the orange juice, water and sugar, and simmer for 10 minutes. Wash and slice the rhubarb into 2 cm pieces. In a separate pan, heat the butter. Add the rhubarb and figs and sauté for 3 minutes.

2 Add the rice and stir to coat. Begin adding the syrup and juice mixture, 1 cup (250 ml, 8 fl oz) at a time, stirring will until liquid is absorbed. Continue to add the syrup in the same manner until all the liquid has been absorbed and the rice is tender. Add the mascarpone cheese and stir well.

3 Cut the fresh figs in half and sprinkle a little brown sugar on each cut surface. Grill the fruit, sugar side up, about 2 minutes until caramelised. Serve atop the risotto in individual bowls.

almond rice jelly

ingredients

90 g (3 oz) ground rice
170 g (5½ oz) ground almonds
60 g (2 oz) powdered gelatine
170 g (5½ oz) castor sugar
60 g (2 oz) dessicated coconut
1.2 litres (2 pints) boiling water
few drops of almond essence (extract)
200 g (7 oz) can lychees
250 g (8 oz) strawberries

serves 6-8

i

preparation time
5 minutes

cooking time
10 minutes

**nutritional value
per serve**
fat: 13.3 g
carbohydrate: 28 g
protein: 9.6 g

1 Into a saucepan, place ground rice, almonds, gelatine, sugar and coconut and mix to combine. Add, while stirring, the boiling water. Bring to the boil and simmer, still stirring for 10 minutes until thick. Stir in almond essence.

2 Pour into a lightly-greased fluted mould, cool, cover and refrigerate.

3 Unmould the rice jelly onto a plate. Garnish with lychees and strawberries.

caramelised rice pudding with apricots

ingredients

75 g (2¹/₂oz) short-grain rice
200 g (7 oz) castor sugar
2 vanilla pods, 1 split in half lengthways
2 tablespoons unsalted butter
600 ml (1 pint) full-fat milk
145 ml (5 fl oz) double cream
2 strips lemon rind (zest)
250 g (8 oz) dried apricots
2 tablespoons lemon juice
1-2 tablespoons cointreau
serves 4

1 Into a saucepan, put the rice and cover with water. Boil for 5 minutes and drain. Return the rice to the saucepan with 45 g (1¹/₂ oz) sugar, 1 of the vanilla pods, butter and milk. Simmer for 45–60 minutes, stirring often, until thickened. Transfer to a bowl and cool for 20 minutes or until cold. Remove the vanilla pod and scrape the seeds into the rice. Discard the pod. Whisk the cream until it forms soft peaks, then fold into the rice.

2 Meanwhile, put 100 g (3¹/₂ oz) of the sugar into a saucepan with the lemon, remaining vanilla pod and 200 ml (7 fl oz) of water. Heat, stirring, until the sugar dissolves. Add the apricots and cook for 10–15 minutes until syrup has thickened. Stir in the lemon juice and liqueur, stand to cool for 5 minutes.

3 Divide the apricots and their syrup between 4 ramekins. Top with the rice pudding and refrigerate for 1 hour. Preheat the grill to high. Sprinkle the puddings with the rest of the sugar. Grill for 1–2 minutes, until the sugar caramelises. Remove and stand 5 minutes to cool before serving.

i

preparation time
10 minutes, plus
1 hour cooling

cooking time
60 minutes

nutritional value per serve
fat: 8.7 g
carbohydrate: 30 g
protein: 2.8 g

glossary

al dente: Italian term to describe pasta and rice that are cooked until tender but still firm to the bite.

bake blind: to bake pastry cases without their fillings. Line the raw pastry case with greaseproof paper and fill with raw rice or dried beans to prevent collapsed sides and puffed base. Remove paper and fill 5 minutes before completion of cooking time.

baste: to spoon hot cooking liquid over food at intervals during cooking to moisten and flavour it.

beat: to make a mixture smooth with rapid and regular motions using a spatula, wire whisk or electric mixer; to make a mixture light and smooth by enclosing air.

beurre manié: equal quantities of butter and flour mixed together to a smooth paste and stirred bit by bit into a soup, stew or sauce while on the heat to thicken. Stop adding when desired thickness results.

bind: to add egg or a thick sauce to hold ingredients together when cooked.

blanch: to plunge some foods into boiling water for less than a minute and immediately plunge into iced water. This is to brighten the colour of some vegetables; to remove skin from tomatoes and nuts.

blend: to mix 2 or more ingredients thoroughly together; do not confuse with blending in an electric blender.

boil: to cook in a liquid brought to boiling point and kept there.

boiling point: when bubbles rise continually and break over the entire surface of the liquid, reaching a temperature of 100°C (212°F). In some cases food is held at this high temperature for a few seconds then heat is turned to low for slower cooking. See simmer.

bouquet garni: a bundle of several herbs tied together with string for easy removal, placed into pots of stock, soups and stews for flavour. A few sprigs of fresh thyme, parsley and bay leaf are used. Can be purchased in sachet form for convenience.

caramelise: to heat sugar in a heavy-based pan until it liquefies and develops a caramel colour. Vegetables such as blanched carrots and sautéed onions may be sprinkled with sugar and caramelised.

chill: to place in the refrigerator or stir over ice until cold.

clarify: to make a liquid clear by removing sediments and impurities. To melt fat and remove any sediment.

coat: to dust or roll food items in flour to cover the surface before the food is cooked. Also, to coat in flour, egg and breadcrumbs.

cool: to stand at room temperature until some or all heat is removed, eg, cool a little, cool completely.

cream: to make creamy and fluffy by working the mixture with the back of a wooden spoon, usually refers to creaming butter and sugar or margarine. May also be creamed with an electric mixer.

croutons: small cubes of bread, toasted or fried, used as an addition to salads or as a garnish to soups and stews.

crudite: raw vegetable sticks served with a dipping sauce.

crumb: to coat foods in flour, egg and breadcrumbs to form a protective coating for foods which are fried. Also adds flavour, texture and enhances appearance.

cube: to cut into small pieces with six even sides, eg, cubes of meat.

cut in: to combine fat and flour using 2 knives scissor fashion or with a pastry blender, to make pastry.

deglaze: to dissolve dried out cooking juices left on the base and sides of a roasting dish or frying pan. Add a little water, wine or stock, scrape and stir over heat until dissolved. Resulting liquid is used to make a flavoursome gravy or added to a sauce or casserole.

degrease: to skim fat from the surface of cooking liquids, eg, stocks, soups, casseroles.

dice: to cut into small cubes.

dredge: to heavily coat with icing sugar, sugar, flour or cornflour.

dressing: a mixture added to completed dishes to add moisture and flavour, eg, salads, cooked vegetables.

drizzle: to pour in a fine thread-like stream moving over a surface.

egg wash: beaten egg with milk or water used to brush over pastry, bread dough or biscuits to give a sheen and golden brown colour.

essence: a strong flavouring liquid, usually made by distillation. Only a few drops are needed to flavour.

fillet: a piece of prime meat, fish or poultry which is boneless or has all bones removed.

flake: to separate cooked fish into flakes, removing any bones and skin, using 2 forks.

flame: to ignite warmed alcohol over food or to pour into a pan with food, ignite then serve.

flute: to make decorative indentations around the pastry rim before baking.

fold in: combining of a light, whisked or creamed mixture with other ingredients. Add a portion of the other ingredients at a time and mix using a gentle circular motion, over and under the mixture so that air will not be lost. Use a silver spoon or spatula.

glaze: to brush or coat food with a liquid that will give the finished product a glossy appearance, and on baked products, a golden brown colour.

grease: to rub the surface of a metal or heatproof dish with oil or fat, to prevent the food from sticking.

herbed butter: softened butter mixed with finely chopped fresh herbs and re-chilled. Used to serve on grilled meats and fish.

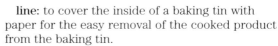

hors d'ouvre: small savoury foods served as an appetiser, popularly known today as 'finger food'.

infuse: to steep foods in a liquid until the liquid absorbs their flavour.

joint: to cut poultry and game into serving pieces by dividing at the joint.

julienne: to cut some food, eg, vegetables and processed meats into fine strips the length of matchsticks. Used for inclusion in salads or as a garnish to cooked dishes.

knead: to work a yeast dough in a pressing, stretching and folding motion with the heel of the hand until smooth and elastic to develop the gluten strands. Non-yeast doughs should be lightly and quickly handled as gluten development is not desired.

line: to cover the inside of a baking tin with paper for the easy removal of the cooked product from the baking tin.

macerate: to stand fruit in a syrup, liqueur or spirit to give added flavour.

marinade: a flavoured liquid, into which food is placed for some time to give it flavour and to tenderise. Marinades include an acid ingredient such as vinegar or wine, oil and seasonings.

mask: to evenly cover cooked food portions with a sauce, mayonnaise or savoury jelly.

pan-fry: to fry foods in a small amount of fat or oil, sufficient to coat the base of the pan.

parboil: to boil until partially cooked. The food is then finished by some other method.

pare: to peel the skin from vegetables and fruit. Peel is the popular term but pare is the name given to the knife used; paring knife.

pith: the white lining between the rind and flesh of oranges, grapefruit and lemons.

pit: to remove stones or seeds from olives, cherries, dates.

pitted: the olives, cherries, dates etc, with the stone removed, eg, purchase pitted dates.

poach: to simmer gently in enough hot liquid to almost cover the food so shape will be retained.

pound: to flatten meats with a meat mallet; to reduce to a paste or small particles with a mortar and pestle.

simmer: to cook in liquid just below boiling point at about 96°C (205°F) with small bubbles rising gently to the surface.

skim: to remove fat or froth from the surface of simmering food.

stock: the liquid produced when meat, poultry, fish or vegetables have been simmered in water to extract the flavour. Used as a base for soups, sauces, casseroles etc. Convenience stock products are available.

sweat: to cook sliced onions or vegetables, in a small amount of butter in a covered pan over low heat, to soften them and release flavour without colouring.

conversions

measurements differ from country to country, so it's important to understand what the differences are. This Measurements Guide gives you simple 'at-a-glance' information for using the recipes in this book, wherever you may be.

Cooking is not an exact science – minor variations in measurements won't make a difference to your cooking.

equipment

There is a difference in the size of measuring cups used internationally, but the difference is minimal (only 2–3 teaspoons). We use the Australian standard metric measurements in our recipes:

1 teaspoon ....5 ml	1 tablespoon....20 ml
1/2 cup......125 ml	1 cup.....250 ml
4 cups...1 litre	

Measuring cups come in sets of one cup (250 ml), 1/2 cup (125 ml), 1/3 cup (80 ml) and 1/4 cup (60 ml). Use these for measuring liquids and certain dry ingredients.
Measuring spoons come in a set of four and should be used for measuring dry and liquid ingredients.
When using cup or spoon measures always make them level (unless the recipe indicates otherwise).

dry versus wet ingredients
While this system of measures is consistent for liquids, it's more difficult to quantify dry ingredients. For instance, one level cup equals: 200 g of brown sugar; 210 g of castor sugar; and 110 g of icing sugar.

When measuring dry ingredients such as flour, don't push the flour down or shake it into the cup. It is best just to spoon the flour in until it reaches the desired amount. When measuring liquids use a clear vessel indicating metric levels.

Always use medium eggs (55–60 g) when eggs are required in a recipe.

dry

metric (grams)	imperial (ounces)
30 g	1 oz
60 g	2 oz
90 g	3 oz
100 g	3 1/2 oz
125 g	4 oz
150 g	5 oz
185 g	6 oz
200 g	7 oz
250 g	8 oz
280 g	9 oz
315 g	10 oz
330 g	11 oz
370 g	12 oz
400 g	13 oz
440 g	14 oz
470 g	15 oz
500 g	16 oz (1 lb)
750 g	24 oz (1 1/2 lb)
1000 g (1 kg)	32 oz (2 lb)

liquids

metric (millilitres)	imperial (fluid ounces)
30 ml	1 fl oz
60 ml	2 fl oz
90 ml	3 fl oz
100 ml	3 1/2 fl oz
125 ml	4 fl oz
150 ml	5 fl oz
190 ml	6 fl oz
250 ml	8 fl oz
300 ml	10 fl oz
500 ml	16 fl oz
600 ml	20 fl oz (1 pint)*
1000 ml (1 litre)	32 fl oz

*Note: an American pint is 16 fl oz.

oven
Your oven should always be at the right temperature before placing the food in it to be cooked. Note that if your oven doesn't have a fan you may need to cook food for a little longer.

microwave
It is difficult to give an exact cooking time for microwave cooking. It is best to watch what you are cooking closely to monitor its progress.

standing time
Many foods continue to cook when you take them out of the oven or microwave. If a recipe states that the food needs to 'stand' after cooking, be sure not to overcook the dish.

can sizes
The can sizes available in your supermarket or grocery store may not be the same as specified in the recipe. Don't worry if there is a small variation in size—it's unlikely to make a difference to the end result.

cooking temperatures	°C (celsius)	°F (fahrenheit)	gas mark
very slow	120	250	1/2
slow	150	300	2
moderately slow	160	315	2-3
moderate	180	350	4
moderate hot	190	375	5
	200	400	6
hot	220	425	7
very hot	230	450	8
	240	475	9
	250	500	10

index